# THE VIEW FROM PISGAH

*A Study in Transfiguration*

Alan Gray

MINERVA PRESS

LONDON

MIAMI   RIO DE JANEIRO   DELHI

THE VIEW FROM PISGAH: *A Study in Transfiguration*
Copyright © Alan Gray 2001

ISBN  0  75411  593  3

First Published 2001 by
MINERVA PRESS
315–317 Regent Street
London W1B 2HS

Printed in Great Britain for Minerva Press

# THE VIEW FROM PISGAH
*A Study in Transfiguration*

*To the memory of the Reverend George Brunskill, one-time New Testament Lecturer at Lichfield Theological College, under whom I served my title in the Parish of Sampford Peverell.*

# Acknowledgements

Philip Sherrard, *Human Image: World Image*, 1992

H V Morton, *In Search of Ireland*, Methuen, 1930

Kenneth E Kirk, *The Vision of God*, abridged ed., James Clarke & Co., 1934, fourth edition, 1977

Paul Verghese, *The Joy of Freedom*, 1967

Thomas Traherne, *The Way to Blessedness*, 1675, ed. Margaret Bottrall, Faith Press, 1962

Quotations from the Holy Scripture are taken from the Jerusalem Bible, 1966.

# Prologue

More than ninety years ago a young man born, bred and educated in Oxford was ordained deacon by the Bishop of Birmingham, Charles Gore. Having obtained a Master of Arts degree he had been offered, but also rejected, an attractive opportunity of a career in astronomy at the Cape Observatory, South Africa. Strangely, as it now seems, his training for Holy Orders comprised no more than a course of reading, followed by a written examination set by the Bishop of Oxford.

The young deacon served his title in the parish of Coleshill with Marston Green. An Evangelical by upbringing, the young and zealous assistant curate used to make an annual attendance at the Keswick Convention. He was surprised to notice that at Coleshill it was not customary to observe the Feast of the Transfiguration of our Lord. Thus, following his ordination to the priesthood, he asked the Vicar whether he might announce a celebration of the Holy Communion on that day, 6 August. The young priest was surprised, not so much that his request was approved, but at the following rejoinder, 'Don't expect to see me there.' There were, I believe, four communicants. The reference is to my father.

Thirty years later my father, then Rector of Pencombe, near Bromyard, was celebrant in his parish church on the Feast of the Transfiguration, with myself as server. It was a memorable occasion for both of us, and for me a kind of itinerarium or blessing, being about to set out on a life-long journey two days later, entering Lichfield Theological College to begin my training for the priesthood. I was ordained deacon in Exeter Cathedral in 1941 and was priested eight months later on the day following my twenty-fourth birthday and in the parish church of Sampford Peverell, being the only candidate.

The curricula vitae of both father and son are left intentionally incomplete. Briefly, however, the record shows that, whereas the call to the priesthood of the father caused him to abandon an opportunity of working in Africa, the son's sent him there to work as a trekking priest.

None of this, though, should be allowed to be distractive or obscurative of that which is of paramount importance – the centrality of the Christ's Transfiguration in the contemplative and active life of every Christian man and woman that is implicit in the experiences of both father and son.

The historical, visionary hill-top experience that follows is offered as a thanksgiving for the privilege of receiving a priestly vocation and for a life that, despite some long wilderness years, has borne much fruit and has been rewarded with some intellectual insights into that Peace which passes all human understanding.

Alan Gray
Malvern
July 2000

# Contents

# INTRODUCTION

This exercise in Christology and Transfiguration makes no claim to scholarship in the full academic sense. It is not intended primarily for scholars, but for the Christian laity generally. My formal education did not begin until the age of ten and a half when I was sent to the local grammar school. To be told you could do better when you think you're trying your hardest is very discouraging. With hindsight, this unhappy experience is seen to reflect at least as much, if not more, on the standard of teaching as upon the ability of the student. Fortunately, the subjects of English, Greek and Geography were well taught, and brought the rewards of School Certificate passes. This acronymic 'EGG' has served as an adequate tripod upon which to begin and sustain what has proved to be a very full and active life. The student's hunger for creative learning has continued unabated, even into the ninth decade of my life. The joy of learning came with the discovery and study of theology.

We are living today in an environment that, from a Christian point of view, is largely alien to the truths upon which our way of life is founded.

The history of the Church of England is, roughly speaking, coincident with the Renaissance and the subsequent Ages of Enlightenment and Romanticism, out of which the Industrial Revolution emerged. During that time and afterwards, the advance of science, mechanisation, technology and various systems of communication have developed to such a degree and with so much impulsion that the Christian Church in this country and in the Western world at large is regarded by many as irrelevant. Of this there is no lack of awareness generally, but in the Church of England it may not be so readily agreed that we have failed to keep pace with this industrial development. We have failed to interpret the Gospel of Jesus Christ in terms that make it relevant. This does not mean that, in any sense, we have to adapt or moderate our Lord's teaching in order to meet the needs of this present generation halfway.

In general terms, what has happened to us as a people is not in the first instance a loss of religion, although that is so for the majority, but a loss of humanity. Mechanisation has debased us, made us superficial, even ridiculous. As a people, our deepest needs, whether we know it or not, will not be met, for example, by persistent, invasive commercialism – whether it is with junk mail, or by means of television, phone or personal caller. Advertisement by television is often seductive and degrading to the dignity, not only of the viewers, but also of the agent acting on the screen. We have become so subject to the consequent effects of industrialism, both at work and at home, that we are making ourselves irrelevant and, in a sense, useless. We don't need to be told repeatedly to 'spoil ourselves', when we already have; nor that, of a certain thing, we 'deserve' it, when we don't. It is precisely because we have made ourselves idle (we call it raising the quality of life) that so many are unemployed or unemployable.

Not so long after arriving in Zimbabwe fifty years ago I discovered that, having succumbed ourselves to the modern dualistic philosophy, we had exported it as well. One afternoon, for some light relief and dressed in khaki shorts and a bush shirt, I took a garden fork to clean some weeds from a flower bed. Hardly had I started than a well-educated, suave African office clerk emerged, saying, 'Father, you don't have to do this; I can get a "boy" to do it for you.' The Bantu clerk, as a white-collar worker, no doubt thought it was infra dig for a priest to be doing so menial a task.

If you lose the sense of what it means to be human you will not see the relevance of religion. We cannot truly know what it means to be human unless we know what is meant by Jesus being the Christ, the truly God–truly man person. Christology teaches us what that means; transfiguration is what happens to us in becoming Christlike.

# THE VIEW FROM PISGAH

That there should be anything at all in common between Malvernians, ancient and modern, and the Moabites, the Middle Eastern tribe of Old Testament history, is improbable but nevertheless true from one aspect. The common factor is a comparable geomorphological feature – a range of bald hills from the high points of which a panoramic view of land near and far, covering the four quarters of the compass, is obtainable.

About two millennia before Moses stood on Pisgah, a beacon of the mountains of Nebo in the land of Moab, Iron Age man was inhabiting the southern beacon of the Malvern Hills. About twelve hundred years before the birth of Christ and after forty years of nomadic life in the wilderness, the Israelites were about to cross the river Jordan and enter the land promised them by God. Before so doing, Moses, like any wise leader, made the ascent of Pisgah to take a look, only to be told by God that he was to go no further and that he must hand over the leadership to Joshua.

The reason for this change of leadership appears to be not on account of Moses' age but, in the opinion of the compilers of Deuteronomy, because he had broken faith with God at Meribath-kadesh. That there is another reason, both profound and prophetic, is evident only following the birth of Christ.

What is not evident in the first instance is that Moses, the man, and Pisgah, the hill upon which he stood, may be seen as types – Moses of the Christ, and Pisgah of the highest point of our God-given personality, the intellect. Being made in the likeness of God and having body, soul and spirit, we have the potentiality of becoming Christlike, which for each one of us, as we shall discover, is equivalent in its effect to a transfiguration. Our intellect is the 'Pisgah' of our personality which enables us to recognise the Christ and also ourselves in His purpose. Thus we shall be enabled to bear witness to the Christian values of truth and justice, mercy and peace; and thus, blessed with purity of heart we shall see God in the face of His Son, our Lord Jesus Christ.

Our erstwhile neighbour, Iron Age man, would have had no understanding of revealed religion, but that does not exclude the possibility that he was capable of having a deep sense of spirituality. Indeed, considering our knowledge of the South African Bushman, provided by the late Laurens van der Post, we may conclude that he probably had. The Stone Age culture of these Bushmen had continued during, we presume, many millennia, resisting external influences until the invasion of South Africa by the Europeans, when the Bushmen's Kalahari homeland was violated and exploited as a tourist attraction.

The Israelites, on the other hand, believing in the revelation of God to Abraham, Isaac and Jacob, eventually took possession of the land promised to them by God. Their history, however, was troubled by many inter-tribal battles, and many were led astray from true allegiance to God, worshipping local heathen gods, and thereby becoming guilty of idolatry. A remnant of the Tribe of Judah remained faithful, and from them, when the time was ready, a son of David's line was born to Mary, Incarnate by the Holy Spirit, the God-man, the Christ, whose name all who believe in Him bear.

But what of Christians, called to inherit a heavenly kingdom – the kingdom of God and His Christ? In attempting to answer this, we must largely confine our thinking to Western Christendom, although Christians worldwide cannot but be affected by the pervading influence of our Western ethos. Nevertheless, we note the continuing emphasis in the teaching of the Orthodox Church on the transfiguring of man, and his restoration to a godlike nature or apotheosis. There appears to be little evidence of this within the Church of England. Christians of the modern Western world – that is, of the past four hundred years at least – have gradually and by now largely lost faith in the idea expressed by the psalmist, that 'the earth is the Lord's and all that is therein'. Contrastingly, mediaeval Christians kept faith with the idea of the sacredness of all of God's creation, and that included all things indirectly created by Him using the skill of human hands. Here we should note that even the Stone Age people, pagan though they were, regarded their manufactures with greater reverence than we do with our mass-produced throwaway articles. We, on the other hand, are surrounded by potentially destructive forces; we are deep in the forest and, since light is obscured, it is only with great difficulty that we can keep our sense of direction.

We must return to Moses, standing alone on Pisgah. The Deuteronomic scribes, familiar though they were with the Law, were lacking in prophetic vision and were, therefore, unable to see the whole purpose of God. They could not see Moses, as we can, as the type of the Christ of God. Thus they were unable to understand why God would not allow him to cross over Jordan into the Promised Land. The reason was not lack of stamina, nor failing eyesight, despite his one hundred and twenty years. Holy Scripture records that Moses died 'in the land of Moab, opposite Bethpeor; but to this day no one has ever found his grave' (Deut. 34:5–7). It is truly remarkable that if the Israelites buried him there it seems highly improbable that the burial place of such a man, their leader for forty years, should have been forgotten.

However, concerning the burial of Moses, there are textual differences which could account for the absence of a grave. Whereas the Greek version records that 'they', the Israelites, buried Moses' body, the Hebrew gives 'he', meaning Yahweh (God). This allows for the reasonable conclusion that Moses' grave could not be found simply because there never was a grave. From the Christian point of view what could be more appropriate than that the body of the man who typified the Christ should be translated?

Holy Scripture provides us with precedential evidence of bodily translation. 'Enoch walked with God. Then he vanished because God took him.' (Gen. 5:24 and Heb. 11:5) More familiar is the taking of Elijah, who 'went up to heaven in the whirlwind' (2 Kings 2:12). Within the Christian era, but not recorded in the Scriptures, there is a long-established belief that the body of the Blessed Virgin Mary, Mother of God, was not subjected to corruption, but translated or assumed. If the bodies of these servants of divine revelation were not corrupted, it seems both appropriate and consistent within the divine ordering of events that Moses himself also should have been translated.

# THE VIEW FROM TABOR

Looking now eastwards towards Pisgah, we can see clearly that God's prevention of Moses from leading the Israelites into the land promised to them was on account of a double truth. Not only was Moses, prophetically, the type of the Christ who was to come, but also the land from which he was forbidden was itself yet to be identified. Moses' destiny, therefore, could not be fulfilled until He, whom he typified, became incarnate. Only then could the true identity of the Promised Land be revealed. So we believe God took the body of Moses to Himself until the time was ready.

The Transfiguration affected not only the figure of the Christ, but the three Apostles also. Peter, James and John, the leaders, were taken to Mount Tabor to witness a manifestation of the Christ, conversing with Moses and Elijah. A cloud of glory covered them and, out of it, they heard the voice of the Eternal Father, saying, 'This is My Belovèd Son... Hear Him.'

What occurred on Tabor may be seen as a solemn Liturgy of Initiation, with our Lord Christ as celebrant and Moses and Elijah as deacon and sub-deacon. The ministry of the Word was spoken and sacramental grace was given to the three Apostles, a sacrament of spiritual enlightenment. The Transfiguration confirmed the truth of God's revelation to His ancient people and prepared the way for the Resurrection, looking towards the establishment of the Kingdom of God. It ended with a strict injunction to Peter, James and John to say nothing until after our Lord had risen from the dead.

If we need further confirmation of the thread of unity that runs throughout the Scriptures, we note the words of Moses in his second Deuteronomic discourse. 'Yahweh, your God will raise up for you a prophet like myself, from among yourselves... to him you must listen.' (Deut. 18:15) We recall here the words of St John's Gospel (1:17), 'though the Law was given through Moses, grace and truth have come through Jesus Christ'. Moreover, the Risen Christ Himself, on the road to Emmaus, qualifies Moses as the type of Himself (Luke 24:27).

Within the Anglican Church at least, the significance of the Transfiguration has not, generally, been explained. By tradition it is placed in the Liturgical Calendar in the post-Pentecostal (Trinity) period, and not chronologically within the observance of the Greater Feasts of our Lord's life – of His birth, Epiphany, Passion and death, Resurrection and Ascension. However, the Church of England Liturgical Commission has come to the decision not to alter the date in the Liturgical Calendar on which the Feast of the Transfiguration is observed. The 6 August has traditionally been the date in the West since the fifteenth century and in the East from the fifth or sixth century. But as a separate issue the Commission has recognised that, sequentially, a Gospel reading of the Transfiguration would be proper between the Epiphany and the Resurrection, for which provision has been made in the Lenten or pre-Lenten period. From Christmas to Pentecost we celebrate a season of theophanies within which the Transfiguration is central, both looking back to Christmas and the Epiphany and forward to Easter and Pentecost. We note that the Prayer Book of the Province of South Africa provides fourteen antiphons to the *Venite*, of which the Epiphany and the Trans-figuration share the same:

> The Lord hath manifested his glory;
> O come let us worship.

The theophany on Tabor enabled the Apostles, Peter, James and John, to identify our Lord Jesus, the Christ of God, as He truly was – the second Adam, paradisal man, the first-born of the second Eve. Mary was a pure virgin, by which we mean she was not only *virgo intacta*, but, by special divine dispensation, she was also a woman free of the stain of original sin from the moment of her conception. This provision was necessary since it was not possible that the Son of God should inhabit a human nature that was subject to the Fall. As paradisal woman, her womb was a fitting receptacle of the seed of God implanted by the Holy Spirit.

The holy child she bore was God-man, truly God, truly man, two natures, one divine, one human, each distinct but inseparably united without confusion in one unique person named Jesus; entitled the Christ by virtue of His divine purpose. Mary was well prepared to give Him body; she could not make Him Christ.

However, the identity of Mary's son remained hidden from the Jews and the world for some thirty years, living in Nazareth where, in popular belief, he helped his stepfather in his workshop. Grounds for this may stem from, 'This is the carpenter's son, surely?' (Matt. 13:55). That He was the Messiah, the Christ, did not become apparent until He began teaching. By explicit revelation it was revealed to the Apostle Peter:

> 'You are the Christ, the Son of the living God.'
>
> (Matt. 16:16–17)

Again, significantly, He revealed Himself to a woman of Samaria (John 4:26), thereby breaking with a long-standing tradition of the Jews. Although our Lord was concerned, firstly, with the recovery of the lost sheep of the House of Israel, no human barrier could be allowed to withhold His presence from the nations of the world.

> O REX GENTIUM. O King of nations, and their Desire;
> The Cornerstone who makest both one: Come and
> Save man, whom thou formedst of clay.
>
> (From South African Prayer Book)

Christology is the study of this Messianic person and, by implication, what His presence in the world means to us all. Philip Sherrard has reminded us in his writings of our need to know the Christ if we are truly to know ourselves.

The Christ, by virtue of His Incarnation, is the expressed immanence of God, His immanence being His 'here-and-nowness'. It is a misconception to speak of Him 'coming down', for it carries the suggestion that God created the universe outside of Himself. God cannot be said to have created the universe outside of Himself, since there is nowhere where He is not. But

God is not only to be thought of as immanent, for He is also transcendent. Thus the Christ is the expressed transcendence of God, this being His ability to be absent, or 'not to be' where previously He was. He demonstrated this on several occasions. Two examples suffice. One at the beginning of His Galilean ministry, when He so enraged the Jews in the synagogue with some straight truths about themselves that they took Him out of the town, intending to throw Him off the cliff, but 'He slipped through the crowd and walked away' (Luke 4:29–30). The second occurred in the Temple after He had declared:

> 'I tell you most solemnly before Abraham ever was, I AM.'
> At this they picked up stones to throw at Him; but Jesus hid himself and left the Temple.
>
> (John 8:58–59)

We observe here that the immanence/transcendence pattern in our Lord's life continues with His Resurrection appearances. Moreover, this pattern appears as characteristic of mankind's experience of relationship with God. Recognition of this is evident in the Psalms, and it also corresponds with the light and dark periods in the spiritual lives of Christians. Thus may we say:

> Father, without Your absence we would not seek You;
> without Your Presence we could not find You.

Seeing that we are here concerned with the identity of the Christ and also with our own, we need to remind ourselves that we are named after His Messianic title and not after His name registered at birth. St Luke records, 'It was at Antioch that the disciples were first called Christians' (Acts 11:26). We note that they were not called 'Jesu-ites'. Antioch, in Syria, was the third city of the empire after Rome and Alexandria in Egypt. It was to Antioch that a great many of the disciples fled following the martyrdom of Stephen.

# THE CHRISTIAN CHURCH

Transfiguration is effectively a form of spiritual transformation which, on Tabor, was manifest to the Apostles as it was also to Saul on the road to Damascus; they became changed men. Humanly speaking it is to be seen intellectually as a continuation of God's creation of man. However, as an activity of the Holy Spirit, acting in a more general way, it can change the course of political history. In preparation for the coming of the Christ, not Israel alone, but neighbouring lands were being made ready. The ground upon which the seed of God's Word would be cast had to be good and well tilled, creating a kind of receptive hunger for the seed. Indeed, the parable of the sower may, at least in part, have been determined with this in mind. A brief historical summary follows.

The post-Pentecostal Christian Church spread with phenomenal rapidity, due partly to the fact that it was under attack from its inception; the opposition which our Lord experienced was inherited by the Apostles. There were, however, hidden factors contributory to this dispersion of the Faith. Historically, the first of these had its roots in the Jewish Diaspora or Dispersion which began with the enforced deportations of the Jews in about the eighth century BC to Western Asia, Armenia and Iran. Later, during the period of Roman rule, the Diaspora, most probably on a voluntary basis, extended westwards to Asia Minor, Greece, Egypt and throughout much of the Mediterranean littoral – notably to Italy and Rome. Generally speaking, these Jews remained faithful to their homeland, to the Law and the Temple. However, many within the Western Diaspora came under the influence of Hellenistic culture.

Nevertheless, in a predominantly pagan world, Jewish monotheism and its synagogue worship became an accepted part of local society wherever Jewish communities became established.

Thus, as we know, on his missionary journeys St Paul went first to preach the crucified and risen Christ in the local synagogues; and we note that his ability to speak Greek as well as Hebrew must have been of considerable value.

Clearly, from our vantage point, we can see that the Jewish Diaspora had been no historical accident, but part of a plan, providentially prepared under the guidance of the Holy Spirit, making a way whereon the Christian Faith could spread rapidly, even against much opposition. Consequently, the outpouring of the Holy Spirit on the assembled Apostles, on the day of Pentecost, and the extraordinary, multilingual, glossolalial outburst that followed had its origin in the Diaspora.

The second major factor contributory to the building of a firm foundation upon which the Christian Faith was consolidated came from pagan Greece. As we have already noted with the Jewish Diaspora, so also in this instance, the minds of the classical Greek philosophers, from the fifth century, were being actively and preveniently enlightened by the Holy Spirit, in preparation for Christ's birth.

Plato, in his later *Dialogues*, abandoned his former dualistic theory of mind and matter in favour of a threefold concept of life, thereby allowing for the acceptance of a spiritual content; he was searching for a Higher Good. It is remarkable that the thinking of this enlightened pagan Greek should have provided the framework upon which Christian theology and philosophy became established. In *Human Image: World Image*, Sherrard wrote in the context of sacred cosmology:

> ...there is no major philosopher, from Plato to Berdyaev, and no major poet, from Homer to Yeats, who has not explicitly or implicitly affirmed the kind of cosmology that we now tend to ridicule, repudiate or ignore. (p.6)

Sherrard also notes the importance of Plato's influence, not only on the ancient Greek world, but also on the thinking of Western mediaeval Christianity. However, he remarks:

> ...in the centuries subsequent to the Renaissance we have increasingly lost our sense of living in a sacred universe, and that

this has had disastrous consequences in every sphere of our lives. (ibid. p.11)

In the post-Apostolic Church, over a period of four centuries, the Greek Fathers were foremost in both framing and defending the orthodoxy of the Christian Faith. This, particularly, centred upon the nature of the Incarnate Christ, the God-man, a single person, in whom the divine and human natures were united, without any confusion of either. Thus, it soon became clear that a definitive statement of the Faith was necessary, not only for the purpose of teaching, but also for the defence of the Faith against error or heresy.

Within the Church of England we do not think of ourselves as heretics, though we have been called thus. If we think of heresy at all, it is in terms of theological unorthodoxy, of one kind or another, concerning the Holy Trinity. In this sense, historically, two heretical teachings are recorded within the first five centuries of the Christian era. In the first instance Arius (circa AD 250–336) denied the divinity of the Christ; his teaching was refuted by the Council of Nicea (AD 345), which led to the formulation of the Nicene Creed. He was followed by Nestorius, who died circa AD 451). He emphasised that the Christ had two aspects, one divine, one human. This was taken by some to mean Christ was two persons; called 'Nestorianism', it was a more insidious heresy than that of Arius, and less easy to identify or eradicate; it has reappeared in our own times, though in a different form.

That this is true is not confined within the Church of England but is evident generally, not only in the Western Church, but in our civilisation. We are saying that to a greater or lesser degree we have, albeit unconsciously, ingested mentally a form of Cartesian dualistic philosophy. In plain language this means that we separated God from His works; we no longer see the universe as sacred. In Orthodox thinking the Christ of God is at the very heart of Creation; if we continue to exclude Him from it we may find, in effect, that we are tolling the death knell of our civilisation.

If we follow this tenet of Orthodox belief we find that the Scriptural account of the Creation may be seen as a series of incarnations or as one incarnation in an evolving, creative work. We recall the words in the prologue of St John's Gospel, 'through Him all things came to be, not one thing had its being but through Him'. Thus we see the very cosmos itself as an incarnation of an idea in the mind of Almighty God.

We cannot but wonder at these things, contemplating the omniscience and love of our Eternal Father. Eternal love alone would make mankind in similarity to Himself, knowing full well His creation would seek to reject that similarity and abuse the authority over the whole created order conferred upon them, claim it for their own and ravage it to the point when it can no longer sustain human life – for that is what is happening today.

Our wondering deepens in consideration of the reality that our Eternal Father made us as He did; for had He not so made us gods in similarity to Himself we would have been in more dire straits than we are, for it would not have been possible for the Son of God to become our Incarnate Saviour. This world is our Egypt, the Christ of God the true Moses, our leader to the eternal kingdom. As we follow in His presence a transfiguration takes place so that we, too, become Christlike.

We note here that the common name for God in the Hebrew tongue is *Elohim*, the plural form. The early fathers saw this as suggestive of the Trinity and therefore of man's own nature. Man is not a monad, a single organism. The likeness does not imply equality, but as we have said, similarity, comprising a trinity of body, mind and soul. Our ability to communicate with our Maker resides in the intellect, the peak of our mind, a unique and saving quality. God made us incarnate that, in the fullness of time, we might be one with Him. If we do not see ourselves as sacred, how then can we so see the universe?

Significantly the teaching of Irenaeus, one of the most influential second-century theologians, held the belief that man, *as conceived in the mind of God*, did not yet exist; that the history of man is one of ascent, a continuing evolution or transfiguration towards divinisation, when we shall stand in the presence of God. Thus, following Irenaeus we may conceive our transfiguration during this earthly life to be a spiritual gestation *in utero aeternitatis*.

# TODAY

Today, if you will hear His Voice, the Voice of His Word, the Christ of God. 'Today, you will be with Me in Paradise.' This second utterance from the Cross was directed, not to a righteous Jew, a Nicodemus, looking for the Kingdom of God, but to a penitent, sinful one; to a man who had been sentenced to death on the cross for stealing. What unbelievable joy he must have felt! Not merely forgiven for his penitence, but much, much more. He received the promise of a place in Paradise that very day. The Christ or paradisal God-man promised this penitent thief restoration to his original status as a human being; his manhood thus restored to equality with the manhood of the God-man on the Cross beside him. This was a moment, we should not forget, that was shared by the mother, watching and waiting below, beside the beloved disciple.

We may meditate on the fact that the penitent thief knew the value of the offer promised him. Such is the condition of our modern society that the self-same offer made today to thieves, robbers and others of antisocial habits would be more likely received with incredulity, derision and obscenity.

The titles Paradisal Man and God-Man, used repeatedly of the Christ, serve to remind us of our origin, being made in His image. The Incarnation of our Lord Jesus Christ is, therefore, both a reminder of and a guarantee of the nature and purpose of the human species within the created order. Affirmation of this is currently necessary, as the following, incidentally, shows. Whenever the opportunity occurs on public broadcasting, the blasphemous assertion that we are descended from apes continues to be made. Presented as though it were common knowledge, it nevertheless appears to go unchallenged; an indication that we, as a people, have accepted the word of science as the word of truth. There need be no objection to the Darwinian theory when applied to the beasts of field and forest, or those of air or water, nor, indeed, to a form of evolution of the human species, for example in stature and facial expression. A primary example is to be found among the South African Bushmen who have physical features which may well be unique to humankind; the reference being to their male and female genitals. We note also that the process of our own transfiguration to Christlikeness is, spiritually speaking, an evolving one.

It is probable that the great majority of Christian people view the account of the Creation as an allegory, a symbolical description. We can assume that the authorship is priestly, since God is said to have rested on the seventh day.

What is noticeable is the orderly development of the Creation, concluding with the making of the human species – a godlike order of being, paradisal figures in stature and bearing; their purpose being to act on behalf of their Creator to oversee the whole created order.

However, there is today evidence of an ongoing form of devolution or, in the light of God's purpose for our species, dehumanisation. Positively, the less Christlike we are, to that extent our human nature falls short of its true potential image. The evidence of this is to be seen in the breaking down of human relationships and in societal misbehaviour, which is largely attributable to the effect on humanity of scientific materialism and the wealth that flows therefrom. The principal sufferers are often the children. There is a cruel irony in the following suggestion, that when Social Services are having to deal with child abuse in homes, they might, with advantage, include a video illustrating the evident tenderness of apes towards their offspring.

# SCRIPTURAL POWER LINES

St Luke's account of our Lord's journey from Jerusalem to Emmaus on the very afternoon of the day of His Resurrection from the dead, accompanied by two disciples, is tantalising. It is left to the reader to do the research, but is sufficient encouragement for students of Christology and members of the Christian laity, generally, to begin searching, beginning with Moses and the prophets.

Tracing the Christological line through the Scriptures is, in some respects, like discovering the electrical layout in a new house. We may extend the similarity further, for an electrical circuit consists, not of one line, but two – one positive, one negative. So it is with Scriptural power lines; in which case, the red, positive, is the Christological, where the black, negative, is none other than the sin of the world.

To assist us in tracing these lines, we may find help by continuing in the context of electricity. If we try to envisage the whole Scriptural revelation as being in the form of a series of transparencies, from Genesis to the Revelation of St John, the transparencies will overlay each other exactly. Thus with some imagination and, as it were, the aid of a simple intermediate technological device, the overhead projector, we shall be able to trace the two lines throughout their whole exposed, revealed, course. In this instance, however, the powerful light is the Light of the Holy Spirit.

The last transparency is of the Revelation of St John, where he records a vision of 'war in heaven'. The Archangel Michael is seen to be defending the Angelic Host from Satan, a rebellious Archangel, who is defeated. He is cast out and enters the created order to become the Arch-tempter of the human race. This provides us with grounds for understanding the behaviour of Adam and Eve in the Garden of Eden.

There is no need to exclude the belief that the human species may have been generated by one original man and one original woman, whilst at the same time accepting the Genesis account of the Creation as an allegory. Thus we see the whole purpose of Almighty God being to place overseers of the created order – a godlike species rendering service to their Creator. As godlike stewards it was necessary they would have freedom to make decisions – a freedom of choice. However, given that, they became vulnerable and lawful prey of the predator of the souls of mankind.

The Tree of Knowledge in the Garden of Eden served as a reminder to Adam and Eve of the sacredness of the whole created order. By yielding to the temptations of Satan, they did despite to the law of sacredness and abused the authority given them. We may see them, therefore, as the aboriginal entrepreneurs or property developers.

There is Scriptural evidence, pre-Christian and Christian, that leads us to believe that, in some sense, the Eternal Father does use the Devil, even bargaining with him. The biography of the man Job begins with a suggestion that his integrity towards God is suspect; that he would renounce God if deprived of his possessions. Thus Satan was allowed a free hand with regard to these, but was restricted from laying a finger on the man himself. Job, however, remained faithful and was duly rewarded.

When the Christ, the Lamb of God came to rescue the human race, although born full of grace and righteousness, that is, 'not born in sin', He was nevertheless subject to temptation. These temptations were real, far more severe than we can imagine, yet He sinned not.

On a much later occasion our Lord's words to Simon Peter at the time of the Passion are indicative of a similar interpretation:

> 'Simon, Simon! Satan, you must know, has got his wish to sift you all like wheat; but I have prayed for you, Simon, that your faith may not fail and once you have recovered, you in your turn must strengthen your brothers.'

> (Luke 22:31–32)

The need of a regular and prayerful reading of the Holy

Scriptures is seen as an essential part of the practice of the Christian way of life. It brings us face to face with a living knowledge of the Christ and of the understanding of His purpose. Generally speaking, our forebears set the modern generation a good example, as the following event in the history of the Mirfield Community reveals.

In 1909, Cosmo Gordon Lang, then Archbishop of York, visited the Community of the Resurrection in order to address a gathering of men in the Quarry (a natural feature in the grounds) used for large assemblies. The men came from within the Diocese of Wakefield, being members of the Bible Reading Fellowship; in all they numbered two thousand! Most probably they would have represented a cross-section of society: miners, mill-workers, railwaymen, office clerks and businessmen.

It is safe to say that these would have been proud of their association with the Bible Reading Fellowship. At that time many millions of householders and cottage dwellers, young and old, would read their Bibles daily. Today we live in a vastly different world, one that is largely indifferent to the Christian way of life. Thus, we find that, apart from the active minority in the Church, the nominally Christian majority today would probably be embarrassed to let their colleagues or workmates know that they read their Bibles; yet, as we learn from the Christian Scriptures, at the time they could do no other than proclaim the things they had seen and heard.

Sixty years ago, even a bus conductor seemed to have caught the spirit of those times. The House of the Resurrection stands on high ground outside the town of Mirfield, on the Huddersfield–Dewsbury bus route. Travellers to the House would probably have made the final stage of their journey by bus, there being a regular service between the two towns, with an official stop near the entrance. By comparison, for example, with a passenger travelling westwards down Oxford Street, hearing the conductor call out in confident Cockney, 'Marble Arch!', our traveller in the north would hear his conductor announce, 'T' Resurrection!' in broad Yorkshire with equal confidence. Our visitor might not have been more surprised if, on reaching the gate, he had been met by the Risen Lord Himself.

The total lack of embarrassment in the conductor's demeanour was refreshing, suggesting that he lived and worked in a more elevated atmosphere than would his kind seem likely to be today. Those who are familiar with H V Morton's *In Search of Ireland* will be reminded of his description of the Irish as showing characteristics of mediaeval Christianity, still unaffected by the destructive forces of materialistic commercialism. Morton wrote of

> ...the delicious slowness of life. Ireland is a Catholic country, and you feel as in most Catholic countries, but notably in Spain, that the material world is rendered unreal and rather childish because it is overshadowed by the spiritual.

We need to remember that Morton was writing at a time when Ireland, and presumably Spain, were both largely unaffected by what he describes as 'the religion of America... the belief in the sanctity of production'. However, to be fair, two points must be observed. First, that the pioneering of the Industrial Revolution was largely attributable to the British, thus it is a shared responsibility. Second, that a large number of the Irish themselves had, by the time of Morton's writing, settled in America, and many of them may have been involved in this production. He went on to say,

> The curse of industrial nations is the cruel and cynical subjection of man to machine. Ireland may be poor, but at least her flesh and blood are not humiliated by that tyranny of mechanical things that is inseparable from the production of wealth.

Needless to say, but sadly so, seventy years later not only the Irish, but many countries around the globe have been submerged by this tidal wave of material greed. We must now attempt to discover how this has come about.

Before we make that attempt, we must investigate the meaning of a third line which runs through the whole of Scriptural revelation. This is the earth line, the line of saving grace. It appears first with the man Noah.

> Noah, a tiller of the soil, was the first to plant the Vine.
>
> (Gen. 9:20)

We are thinking of the vine and the vineyard that was brought out of Egypt; this is an allegory that was first to come true when the infant Christ Child was brought out of Egypt, following the massacre of the infants. The major references in the Old Scriptures are allegorically Messianic:

> Let me sing to my friend the song of his love for his vineyard.
>
> Yes, the vineyard of Yahweh Sabaoth is the House of Israel, and the men of Judah that chosen plant.
>
> (Isa. 5:1, 7)

Later, Israel, having forsaken the purposes of God, were taken into exile; in Psalm 80 they pleaded to be allowed to return.

> Please, Yahweh Sabaoth, relent! Look down from heaven, look at this vine, visit it, protect what your own right hand has planted.
>
> (Psalm 80:14)

Towards the end of his earthly ministry, Jesus the Christ of God, openly declares Himself to be the historical reality of the vine:

> I am the true Vine, and my Father is the vine dresser.
>
> I am the Vine, You are the branches.
>
> (John 15:1, 5)

Finally, our Blessed Lord, knowing that His life on earth was near its end, and having expelled the dealers from the Temple and left the barren fig tree withered, uttered two parables, both concerning vineyards (Matt. 21:28–43). We will confine ourselves to the second. There is a tragic beauty in this, as our Lord tells it of Himself, knowing that His hearers would not understand. His Father, the owner and vine dresser, having already sent the

Prophets to the Israelite stewards, who were roughly treated, sent His own Son, whom they kill. But there was to be a triumphant end to the parable, with the Son's breaking out of the tomb, resurrected from death, then to ascend, majestically, into heaven.

This, however, is a parable with a lasting relevance.

# THE ROOTS OF CRISIS

The Western Church is facing a crisis that is both internal and external, which for the Church of England and the reformed churches as a whole, has developed extensively since the Reformation. Whether the crisis might have been avoided or better controlled had the Western Church not been weakened by the divisions brought about by the Reformation cannot be considered here. As it is, the sacramental materialism of the Christian Church has been endangered by the tide of secular materialism attributable to the Industrial Revolution.

In attempting to understand how this situation came about we must look back several centuries – to the Renaissance. Without this rebirth of ideas there might never have been an Industrial Revolution, or at least we might have been spared the worst effects of it, in human terms. The two mechanised wars of the last century wrought havoc on global society; and in Western society in particular, the religious life has been replaced by the secular in popular thinking.

In mediaeval Europe, education had been, largely, in the hands of the monasteries; but, from the twelfth century onwards, it gradually became independent of them. The foundation of many schools and universities date from this period in our history. From the eighth century the syllabus of elementary education, known as the Trivium ('where three ways meet'), comprised grammar, rhetoric and dialectic which prepared for the Quadrivium, comprising music, arithmetic, geometry and astronomy. Together they were known as the Liberal Arts, and were regarded as an essential preliminary to the study of theology. By the later Middle Ages the majority of students were choosing to further their reading in Medicine and Law. These came to be known as the Lucrative Sciences – the first instance, perhaps, of education being related to material benefit. With the revival of interest in Pythagoras and Euclid, Mathematics became an increasingly important subject.

Fundamentally, a subtle change in the trend of human thinking was taking place, which is usually epitomised in the thinking of the French philosopher and mathematician, René Descartes (1596–1650). His idea of God was of an absolutely perfect being, who, nevertheless, was envisaged as being totally remote from human activity – a concept wholly unacceptable within the Christian Faith. Thus, at the beginning of the eighteenth century – the early years of the Industrial Revolution – the thinking of many intellectuals was based on the Aristotelian/ Cartesian dualistic concept of mind and matter. The secular, dualistic materialism of many scientists and physicists derives from this contributory philosophical development and is evident still.

We must, however, draw attention to the distinction between Christian and secular materialism. The Christian Faith is, avowedly, materialistic. Indeed, it could not be otherwise and remain true to itself. Christian materialism is sacramental and is built upon the fact of the Incarnate Christ, who is Lord of all Creation. He is archetypal, not solely of the human species, but also of the whole created order. This truth is expressed by the Apostle John saying, 'Through Him all things came to be, not one thing had its being but through Him.' (John 1:3) We declare the same in the Eucharistic Creed, saying, that by Him 'all things were made'. Therefore, since the whole created order is of God, all is sacred.

Furthermore, the Gospel of St John is evidential of the beginning, within the Christian Church, of a form of worship that is both sacramental and liturgical. The Sacraments are a constant reminder to us of the sacredness of both people and things. The Son of God, by becoming incarnate, may be seen as a Living Sacrament, the outward and visible sign of the invisibly immanent God, Emmanuel, as foretold by the prophets.

The crisis facing the Christian Church, at the present time, is seemingly not one from which it can escape. We find ourselves living in an environment that, idealistically and politically, is totally foreign to the Christian Faith and its way of life. This does not exclude the possibility that Divine Providence may be permitting it as a way of testing our faith. Even if, internationally, governments are at peace, fighting for the Faith is never an easy-going or comfortable pursuit.

During the past two centuries, especially, the pursuit of wealth in both industry and commerce has been relentless, thereby bringing about a change of ethos in Western society. Thus Western Christians, particularly, find themselves having to survive in an ethos that, idealistically, is totally opposed to the teaching of the Christ, the author of our Faith. We are trying to survive in the world of Mammon. Like the ancient Israelites who tried to combine faith in God with the worship of man-made gods, so are we in danger of having a fascination, that may amount to worship, with the symbols of wealth.

The following two examples come from my own experience; both are explicit and contextually apt. Some years ago a financier decided to put his money into a cause which he considered to be good. In the grounds of his home he built a boarding school for the sons of the financially elite. Customarily he told prospective parents that his advice for pupils to follow in their working lives was to read, habitually, the *Financial Times* at the breakfast table; also that they could consider themselves successful if, by the age of thirty, they had made a million.

More recently, while I was waiting for an appointment, the following heading to an advertisement in a glossy magazine came to my attention:

> WANT, WANT, WANT, WANT, WANT –
> IT'S WHAT THE WORLD IS ALL ABOUT.

Perhaps the extent to which we will go in demonstrating this ethos, is exemplified by the attention given on television to the National Lottery. The ballyhoo and razzmatazz associated with the now twice-weekly draw, in which 'celebrities' are invited to role-play the pimps of Mammon, contributes to the raising of an excitement of the national audience to a frenzy that is reminiscent of a Bacchanalian feast. The Old Testament prophets would not have minced their condemnation, likening it to fornication with a foreign god.

# AN ANGLICAN VIEWPOINT

Speaking generally, the teaching of the Anglican Church conforms to the Western teaching and practice of the Christian Faith. But, as an individual branch of the West, our own teaching and practice has been built upon that of the Apostles and the early Church Fathers, many of whom were Greeks; hence our empathy with the Greek Orthodox Church of modern times.

We note that whilst the term 'orthodox' means that with which there is general agreement, the term 'catholic' means universal. However, following the division of Orthodox East from Catholic West, and particularly during the years following the Counter Reformation, the papacy has effectively given the term 'Catholic' a double meaning. Derivatively separate, the two terms have become virtually synonymous by general agreement of the greatest number. Yet, withstanding this claim, in one vitally important specific the Eastern Orthodox Church may be seen to be more perceptive than Western Christendom – concerning the Incarnation of the Son of God and the Holy Trinity. Whereas in the Western Church we have been inclined towards a belief in the Incarnation as referring, simply, to the conception and birth of our Lord, the Orthodox have a more comprehensive belief. For them, it embraces the whole of our Lord's earthly life.

We would be wholly wrong in seeing this as no more than a difference of emphasis, since the view of the West is deceptively misleading; it has the effect of making the Incarnate Christ appear to be a figure of ancient history, whereas He is in the forefront of our daily lives. We need to have an in-depth rethink. By becoming man, the Son of God, the Christ, stands amongst us as a reminder to the whole human species of His Father's purpose, setting us in a position of authority over the whole created order; He made us lords of His Creation; our original failure in this necessitated the coming of the Christ. On the Cross He died for our failure, but triumphed over death, rising to new life in the

Resurrection; ascending into heaven He took His manhood with Him. By taking His Incarnation into heaven, He has made it a perpetuating truth for all mankind. The Risen Christ is a constant reminder that God made us for Himself – for life eternal; but as we have already noted, man's original fall from grace and his subsequent history have hindered God's original plan of man's deification:

> I once said, 'You too are gods, sons of the Most High, all of you.'
>
> (Psalm 82:6)

That no more than a remnant of the total membership of the Church of England continues to be regular and frequent in attending public worship is now generally evident. But this decline, which began to be noticeable following the end of the Second World War, cannot be attributed to the effects of that alone; nor solely to the undermining effects of liberal materialism in subsequent years. However, the War itself probably acted as the catalyst.

Church historians may, in due time, consider that the root of the problem lay in the structure of the Church of England. It has often been likened to a bridge across a divide that provides access between the opposite sides – Anglo-Catholic and Anglo-Protestant. Whilst these two anchor points are an essential part of the whole construction, it is the bridge that determines its name. Hence the Church of England is called a Broad Church. However, whilst the whole bridge is as much dependent on its anchor points as it is on the design and construction, the analogy is incomplete. The potential strength of the whole structure depends greatly on the quality and strength of the materials used – the members. A survey shows there are signs of weakness in the central section of the bridge.

When we look back over the past three centuries of the history of the Church of England, we see that the Evangelical Revival of the eighteenth and nineteenth centuries and the Anglo-Catholic of the nineteenth and early twentieth centuries had little effect on the Broad Middle, which up to the Second World War constituted the numerical majority. Lacking a corporate identity it had little sense of direction. The Faith, though not abandoned, remained fairly static.

Having worked for twelve years in Southern Africa as a trekking priest, I have believed for some time that the greatest single hindrance to the spiritual growth of the Church of England is its establishment with the State. It is significant that the Church in Wales, which was disestablished in 1920, has subsequently grown in 'influence and numbers' (*Oxford Dictionary of the Christian Church*, ed. F L Cross). In general terms this cannot be said of the Broad Middle of the Church of England, which, lacking a sense of corporate identity, has generally speaking failed, not only to grow numerically, but has visibly declined. By and large membership of this Central Body is representative of prosperous Middle England, and herein lies the greatest conflict of interests. It is this that most frequently hinders the influence which flows from the Holy Spirit, who is the life-force of the Church, the Body of the Christ.

Maintenance is a service industry. This in reality means pastoral care, seemly and orderly conducting of services, with preaching or instructing of the laity. We note that there is evidence of an increasingly committed laity, in some parishes, who both preach and teach. We must not overlook the value of committed lay men and lay women who may often be better able to reach into the hearts and minds of people where a priest, in the first instance, might fail.

For the purposes of this study we draw attention to three factors that appear contributory to declining congregations. First, in the Book of Common Prayer, after the Order of Holy Communion, the rubrics give inadequate and misleading information with regard to the frequency of receiving the Blessed Sacrament of Christ's Body and Blood. Sacramentally speaking, our forebears did not receive an adequately balanced diet. Thus, broadly speaking, it was not until we had the benefit of the Alternative Services currently in use that the Broad Church was encouraged to worship at the Holy Eucharist and receive the spiritual benefits of the Sacrament regularly and more frequently.

Second, there is evidence suggesting that the content of preaching within the Broad Church lacked balance, being too heavily weighted on the side of the social aspects of the Gospel and, especially, on the subject of Christian morality.

More than fifty years ago while serving my title in an united rural benefice, I was often faced with a challenging question, usually made by men, 'You don't have to go to church to be a Christian, do you?' This is now seen as evidence of a lack of religious teaching on the fundamentals of the Christian way of life. The following anecdote is relevant here. A member of the Community of the Resurrection, having an Evangelical or Broad Church background, was commissioned to travel to Rome, probably to attend a conference on Anglo-Roman relationships. It was his first visit and, on account of his background, his impressions were eagerly sought on his return. Having concluded his report on the conference he said, 'What impressed me most was the evidence, generally, of great emphasis being placed upon religion, and yet, so little upon morality.'

This anecdote is not intended to imply that morality in the Christian life is of secondary significance, rather that without a proper grounding in Christian religion, moral behaviour tends to become detached from its foundation. This gives rise to the observation that the Church of England has tendencies towards Nestorianism, whereby the Incarnate Lord is thought of as being not one, but two persons, one human, one divine. This means that, effectively, we follow the human Jesus, who came to make us good, giving us a new set of rules. At the same time we reject or shy off the divine Christ of religion. If we extend this line of thinking we are exposed to the charge of self-centredness, upholding Christian moral teaching simply because it makes common sense; it makes the world a better, safer place for decent people. Little thought is given to the religion that supports the moral code.

To arrive at a fuller understanding of this we need to examine our historical roots. The growth of Renaissance humanism in the fifteenth century drew attention to man's, rather than God's, influence in the world, though at the time it was not seen as representing a challenge to the teaching of the Church. Most probably the undivided Western Church, whilst still affirming the mediaeval belief of the sacredness of the universe, reasoned that man's influence was beneficial. We note that centuries later the dictum of Austin Farrer applies – God makes man make things happen.

But two events were to follow which would eventually have disastrous consequences. Firstly, there is the evidence that the Reformation not only divided but seriously weakened Western Christendom. Secondly, from a Christian viewpoint, the Industrial Revolution effectively undermined the mediaeval concept of a sacred universe.

Arising from this historical background, in more modern times it is evident that Protestantism generally, and the Church of England in particular – being our chief concern – placed too great a reliance upon morality to the exclusion of religion and did, albeit unwittingly, contribute to our present problems. In so doing they prepared an ideal seedbed on which the fungal spores of liberal humanism were able to germinate and spread. This largely immoral form of humanism is not only difficult to control but much harder to eradicate. It ignores or ridicules religion and repudiates belief in the sacred nature of the universe. Furthermore it justifies and substantiates Sherrard's comment that it has 'had disastrous consequences in every sphere of our lives'.

Our knowledge of the Christian religion is founded on revealed truth which we usually think of as reaching us in the form of writing or by word of mouth. However, it can also come in the form of a religious experience. In the context of this work the obvious example is of the three Apostles on Mount Tabor, who witnessed the Transfiguration of the Christ and were themselves transfigured by it. Many instances of truth about God have been revealed in the Scriptures and experienced in the lives of the Saints.

Two examples of Scriptural theophanies are given here. The first of these occurred at the time of the ratification of the Covenant:

> Moses went up with Aaron, Nadab and Abihu, and seventy elders of Israel. They saw the God of Israel beneath whose feet there was, it seemed, a sapphire pavement pure as the heavens

themselves. He laid no hand on these notables of the sons of Israel: they gazed on God. They ate and they drank.

(Exod. 24:9–11)

The second instance, recorded in the Gospel of St Luke, is one of the Resurrection appearances and is significantly comparable. When Jesus appeared to the Apostles He said to them:

'Why are you so agitated, and why are these doubts rising in your hearts? Look at my hands and feet; yes, it is I indeed. Touch me and see for yourselves; a ghost has no flesh and bones as you see I have.' ...Their joy was so great that they still could not believe it... He said to them, 'Have you here anything to eat?'

(Luke 24:38–42)

We note on this occasion that God Incarnate invited the witnesses to touch Him, and it was He who ate in *their* presence.

The evidence that the practice of Christian morality without the observance of Christian religious duties is generally unsustainable is only too apparent, at the present time, with the prevailing decline in moral standards.

There is a strong probability that the prevailing decline in the practice of Christian moral standards is, in some measure, due to our having, over many generations, placed too great an emphasis on morality and too little upon the religious foundation of the Christian life. In other words, our attention has been centred on human relationships, one with another, rather than on our relationship with God; with the last six of the Ten Commandments rather than the first four.

Morality divorced from religion is like a plant uprooted from the ground that gives it life and enables it to grow. It leads to lawlessness; lawlessness leads to godlessness. When the Christ becomes an irrelevance, Christian identity is lost. When identity is lost, prayer, worship and the Sacraments also cease to have any relevance.

This part of our study could not be better concluded than by some quotations from Kenneth E Kirk's *The Vision of God* (abridged edition, 1934).

His great work received the acclaim of Catholics and Protestants alike:

> Ethics, or teaching about man and the conduct proper to him, centres a man's thoughts upon himself; the end of self-centredness is unethical and unevangelical alike. It is bound to result... either in spiritual pride or in spiritual despair: and by neither of these roads can a man find his true destiny. (p.46)

> So far from being a selfish goal, worship is the only way to unselfishness which Christians have at their command. (p.185)

> In worship... worshippers put themselves in an attitude of dependence. In looking towards God, Who is All in All, they see themselves to be nothing; in worshipping the Redeemer they know themselves incapable of redeeming the least of God's creatures. (p.185, edited by the author)

> Worship tells us much good of God, but little good of ourselves, except that we are the work of God's hands. For that we may praise Him, but it leaves us nothing upon which to pride ourselves. (ibid.)

> Disinterested service then is the only service that is serviceable; and disinterestedness comes by the life of worship alone. (p.186)

> The spirit of worship is not a remote prize. It is an actual endowment possessed by all... We are born into a world where we cannot but worship; even if we learn to worship the devil and his works, we shall still retain some trace of the worship of God to the very end. Wherever goodness has attracted the soul, it has evoked the spirit of worship; and it will continue to attract. (p.194)

A brief domestic incident is exemplary of the means whereby God's presence may enter the soul through the gateway of goodness. It is 5 p.m. on a winter evening in 1933. The family of five and a visiting uncle are sitting around the fire; the rest of the house is cold. The invalid mother has occasional need of family support. 'Would one of you like to...?' she asks. Nobody is inclined to leave the comfort of the fire. The uncle offers two shillings as a reward. One of the children offers to go, but declines the reward. At that very moment, through the mother's goodness and her need, an awareness of the presence of God entered that child's soul.

# LITURGY

The word will be familiar to the majority of the laity, though its derivation may not be so. Liturgy is derived from two Greek words which originally – i.e. in pre-Christian times – referred to a public duty, though not necessarily a religious one. The Christian Church adopted the word with reference to the public duty of Eucharistic worship which we in the West have followed. Liturgy, however, is also used to denote the form of words used in performing that duty.

With regard to this, the intention of the Christian Church is to give thanks to God or make Eucharist. The Daily Office, incumbent upon the Clergy, has the same connotation, being known as the opus Dei. Thus, collectively, the liturgical services comprise the works of God and of His people.

By comparison with the attendance figures of fifty years ago, the decline during the subsequent years in the number of worshipping Anglicans has become common knowledge. Whilst a multitude of external forces have been contributory to this decline, insofar as the Church of England is involved, there would seem to be evidence of those forces not being the sole cause.

Until the introduction of the Parish Eucharist some forty years ago, the traditional times of Sunday worship – Holy Communion at 8 a.m., Sung Matins at 11 a.m. and Evensong at 6.30 p.m. – had become stereotyped, particularly in rural parishes. These are now seen to have been divisive and elitist. The Church's principal Liturgy was regularly attended by the few, except on the occasions of the Greater Festivals. The majority of the congregation attended Matins. One has only to read the rubrics following the Order of the Holy Communion in the Book of Common Prayer to discover how the old order of Sunday Services came to be.

If we take into consideration the revision of 1927–28, which was rejected by Parliament, the Book of Common Prayer and its successor, the Alternative, was under revision for the greater part of the twentieth century. To the laity, and perhaps the clergy not directly engaged in it, the process seems lengthy. With historical perspective, we are able to remind ourselves that the Book of Common Prayer (1662), which became our workbook for some two hundred and fifty years, was itself, in a sense, one hundred and thirteen years in preparation. That this revision should take so long is in some measure accountable to the wide diversity of beliefs or opinions spanning the Anglo-Catholic and Anglo-Protestant points of view.

When the process of revision is complete it is to be hoped that priests and laity alike will have a book that fulfils their deepest needs. The book will be judged by its ability in helping us all to worship God better, in the fellowship of our Lord Jesus Christ, in the unity of the Holy Spirit. A common experience, particularly when visiting mediaeval churches, is an awareness of an atmosphere – of a presence – rather like, one imagines, that of a blind person sensing the presence of someone else in the room. What we are discerning is like an accumulation of latent awareness of past generations of worshippers sensing the transcendence of God. In worship it is our awareness of the transcendence of God that makes His presence felt.

We should not suppose that this experience is confined within the walls of a church. When Jacob left Beersheba for Haran, after his first night's sleep, in which he dreamt of a ladder standing between earth and heaven, he said, on wakening, 'How awe-inspiring this place is! This is nothing less than a house of God; this is the gate of heaven' (Gen. 28:17). This exceptional experience of one man on a journey is one which, on rare occasions, might happen to anyone.

Christian Eucharistic worship is essentially a communal act. Paul Verghese, in his *The Joy of Freedom* (1967) wrote against the background of Eastern Orthodox Eucharistic worship. This, in common with all Eucharistic worship, contains, first, a ministry of the Word – the reading of Holy Scripture followed by preaching. What he says of the needs of mankind in the modern world is not confined to the Eastern Orthodox Church but is applicable throughout Christendom. 'Preaching, in measure and with quality may still speak to him...' I shall never forget the example given to theological students of Lichfield Theological College. It was conveyed by quoting the following anecdote.

A young, newly ordained deacon, having joined the staff of a large urban parish, was asked by his Vicar to preach at Evensong the following Sunday. Being a little anxious, he asked, 'What shall I preach about?' The reply was immediate and succinct: 'About God and about twenty minutes.'

If the 'measure' and 'quality' are provided, they will serve as an aid to the worship of God. Preaching can be the aid to divine worship, but never the end, for one clear reason – the hearers are no more than recipients. Worship is a communal act of giving. For this reason Paul Verghese goes on to say, 'but certainly he needs a great deal more'. In the context of the Parish Eucharist that 'great deal more' is seen to be the growing together in an awareness of the presence of God in the Body of His Christ, and in the fellowship of the Holy Spirit; in the presence of the Saints and Angels assisting us, not only in our worship but in our daily living.

The Alternative Eucharistic Rites have helped to 'gather up' our experience of life as we understand it today, so that we can bring it before God. But that is not enough on its own. As Paul Verghese says, summarising, there must be an awareness of the transcendent, which will enable us to experience the 'transcendent unity of the community'. As I see it, this is comparable with H V Morton's experience of the Irish in the 1920s, with whom the material world is made to appear unreal, being overshadowed by the spiritual.

If we are to be able to participate in this awareness of transcendent unity, in communal fellowship, it will be by the gift of God, in response to our attendance upon Him in worship.

We need to recognise that we are, unavoidably, having to live our Christian lives in what is virtually a 'foreign' country, not dissimilar to the experience of the Israelites in exile. We are surrounded by sinister, aggressive forces that consider our beliefs entirely irrelevant. That their views are founded on ignorance presents us with a challenge; our Lord Jesus Christ, our King, has made us His ambassadors, representing Him wherever we are sent.

With hindsight it may be said that we have largely failed to meet that challenge. Some indications have already been given to account for this. More particularly I believe we have been deficient in the field of apologetics, which is a gift of the Spirit. It is a method of Evangelism. The apologist exercises his gift by interpreting the profound truths of the Christian Faith in rational terms that can be readily understood by the laity. I can speak from experience, though I lack the gift myself. Twice, at least, during my time in the Community of the Resurrection and once again a few years ago when on holiday in a West Sussex town, I had the privilege of listening. It is truly an inspiring and uplifting experience – a good palliative when sitting on an uncomfortable pew!

Our Christian Faith is a religion which binds us to God as members of the Body of the Christ of God. If we do not accept the ropes that bind us, and why they are necessary, they may in time become loosened, or we may be tempted to cut them; we shall then be exposed and defenceless against the lures of secular materialism. Surely our best hope for the future must depend upon the training of the children of today.

In this respect I believe we should give serious consideration to the preparation of children for making their First Communion from the age of seven or eight. Initially, this should be allowed only in specific instances and when parental encouragement and support would be given. There are grounds for this on two accounts: firstly, there is continuing precedent in support of this; and secondly, particularly in view of the contentious forces in their environmental upbringing, it is wholly irrational to continue with the existing practice of associating the First Communion with Confirmation, which deprives young children, on entering the age of reason, from the grace that flows from this Blessed Sacrament. It should be apparent that, currently, there are too many and too great pressures on adolescents to allow them to establish the regular custom of making Sacramental Communion. It is not surprising that, over a long period of time, many have not persisted. Preparation for Confirmation would then be given in the middle teens.

Furthermore, under the present practice, it is customary for parents or godparents to give the newly confirmed a Communicant's Manual; in itself a commendable custom. However, it is seen as regrettable that so many of them include the question, 'How often shall I make my Communion?' Such a question seems reminiscent of the Book of Common Prayer rubric advising communicants to receive Holy Communion not less than three times a year. The same question would not be asked of Sunday dinner. What the question in the Manual does is to suggest that the reception, and the frequency of it, is a private or personal matter; whereas it is, institutionally, a communal act, a sacramental meal, the nature of which, ordinarily, is a frequent act.

# A GROUND-LEVEL VIEW

Whether our point of view has been from the Malvern Hills, Pisgah, Tabor, or that indescribable visionary height of the human intellect, the vast majority of us live in the cities, towns or villages on relatively level ground and thither we now return.

The creation of the cosmos and of our small world within it relates to the fullest extent of geological time or the prehistoric. During this unfathomable process, the Infinite creates horizons, the Eternal makes history. In Genesis, the priestly authors wrote that God's final act of creation was to make man in His own image. On the other hand the record of modern biological research leads us to believe that the human species evolved from the apes. Charles Darwin, however, was not qualified to determine the unique nature of man.

Theologically speaking, the obvious similarity, both of the physical appearance and bodily structure of man and ape raises no problems, given the recognition that the essential difference between the two is not detectable by any means of biological research. For, hidden within the rugged and hairy exterior of the original man and woman, the Creator implanted an uniquely wonderful 'seed' – the embryonic conscience – described in Genesis as the tree of knowledge. Thus, alone amongst all living creatures, the human species is endowed with the means of knowing God and having the ability of evaluating between good and evil, right and wrong.

Nevertheless, this God-given faculty also provided for a freedom of expressing a preference, and so gave us the inherent possibility of making a wrong decision. Thus we are said to have been 'born in sin' – a misleading phrase to the uninitiated. It means, simply, that we are born having a capability of doing wrong or being evil. Thus learning not to be selfish, greedy, bad-tempered or covetous are essential lessons of our elementary education.

In theological terms these base human traits are said to be attributable to the fall of man or the 'original sin of man'. We should not, however, envisage these as historical events, such as Adam and Eve, like Humpty Dumpty, having a great fall. We lose nothing by rephrasing it as 'attributable to man's fallibility'.

As we enter upon the third millennia of the Christian era, some may see the events of the past century as fulfilling the prophecy of the Christ Himself, namely the two titanic wars undertaken in defence of the rights of humanity to a freedom of choice in a political context. One thing only is certain: our Lord's warning has been given and will not be repeated.

We need to remember, though, that there is a continuing war in our midst – of international proportions and of a very different type – the aggressive struggle for supremacy and survival among the giants of commerce and industry. Companies embark upon these conflicts in the name of progress and commercial success from which, tragically, there flows an ever-increasing toll of casualties. These include smaller companies that may have been subsidiaries to the greater and those that are independent; but it is the helpless pawns of industry and commerce – the employees – who are the least able to survive, becoming unemployed or unemployable.

However, it must be said of these battlefields referred to above that at least they are visible to the human eye. Having successfully and territorially assisted other countries to free themselves from the invader, and defended our own from invasion, we must beware of becoming complacent. During the past fifty years a more subtle and surreptitious invader of our society has appeared. It is an enemy that could hardly have been anticipated and already much damage has been done; it is a traitor of the 'quisling' type. Liberal humanism is as lethal in Christian terms upon our thinking as is honey-fungus to the forest floor. It has the ability, for example, of occluding or distorting our conception of values when trying to make decisions.

The basic desire of liberated man may be described as the right to have unlimited opportunities of becoming rich and to unrestricted sex; of liberated woman – the desire to escape the domination of men and to have the freedom of acquiring financially rewarding employment with the independence that follows therefrom. In both instances there is an underlying belief that achievement will bring fulfilment and contentment. However, in the case of the woman the bearing of children must not be allowed to impinge upon her freedom; thus with an acquired executive authority she deputises this important task to grandparents or carers.

Readers should note that this somewhat severe assessment comes from a warm-hearted and happily married man.

If what we have described are the principles of liberated men and women in a post-industrial age, they are unacceptable within the teaching of the Christian Church. Most of us are familiar with the notion of making a re-evaluation of our lives from time to time. In the present context we cannot do better than return to the primary questions of the general catechism of the Christian Church:

Q. Who made me?
A. *God* made me.

Q. Why did He make me?
A. He made me for Himself.

We note here that self-appointed liberated man or woman will be inclined to misquote, emphatically, the answer to the first question. Replying to the first question, 'God made *me*,' is tantamount to attributing one's condition to God, which is blasphemous. The same attribution would not be so readily made of one born with Down's syndrome or any other genetic disability.

We also continue within the catechism to state our belief that God made us in His image; thus the Creator makes us creators, or as we say, procreators. As such, therefore, our primary purpose is to procreate children for God's eternal kingdom.

We are now faced with a question not listed in the catechism: 'What makes us desire to procreate?' In a word our loving and eternal Father has equipped us with a faculty which is characteristically erotogenic – a single source of creative energy essential for the procreation and upbringing of children. Whilst

51

noting these truths within the context of a Christian study, we must not overlook the truth of their being universally applicable to mankind whatever their beliefs.

But sadly it is evident in our modern society that the ragged edges of human fallibility become exposed. One of the most regrettable and unhappy effects of liberal humanism has been the growth of sexual permissiveness. On the one hand it undermines the stability of marital harmony and, on the other, it encourages and accommodates homosexuality. The latter particularly strikes at the heart of the divinely ordered erotogenic plan of procreation. Furthermore, sexual deviancy and permissiveness has historically been one of the primary indicators of societal decadence.

My choice of words is deliberate; but we must not overlook the reality that anyone entering into a relationship involving acts of sexual deviancy becomes responsible for the perversion of natural law established by God for man. Adultery, on the other hand, is a sin in the sight of God, though it does not constitute a violation of natural law in the nature of the act.

There can be no doubt but that liberal humanism has seriously confused the issue. Whilst it is evident that homosexuality is a genetic disorder there is little evidence, in Christian terms, of the reality that the grace of God is sufficient. Claiming a human right to be a deviant will only obstruct this saving grace.

In a study that has been occasionally overtly speculative we question, in the light of man's erotogenic faculty, whether there is a link between the prevalence of homosexuality and a sense of deprivation caused by, or exacerbated by, the inability to find and develop innate creative skills that can lead to a fulfilling occupation.

When taking a ground-level view of the human world as it is today, reference to this unhappy subject could hardly be avoided, since it is fundamental to the view of human self-image, worth and dignity – all in the light of our eternal destiny. Christian man, we should remember, takes his identity from the Christ. At the gate of heaven our identity will be the passport to recognition and admission.

# EPILOGUE

This brief and sometimes speculative study owes much to the scholarship of others, both ancient and modern. A general understanding of the creation of the cosmos and the whole created order of living things, of creatures and especially of man, is also indebted to the research, in modern times, of archaeologists and physical scientists.

Theologians and scriptural exegetes, acknowledging the value of these inputs, are thus able to view the account of the Creation in Genesis with the advantage of a visionary, hill-top, prehistorical perspective. We may reflect that if Noah had been given a similar advantage he might have feared for the safety of his craft and all within it if *Tyrannosaurus rex* and *regina* had appeared looking for an escape from the Flood.

The translation of Holy Scripture into the vernacular has given people of virtually every race and nation the opportunity of reading and studying the Bible. However, it is safe to say that a great many who have responded were unlikely to have had the advantage of the Ethiopian eunuch who, fortuitously, had the benefit of an interpreter. The lack of qualified interpreters, coupled with the mistaken belief that the Bible is none other than the *ipsissima verba* of God, has contributed to many adopting fundamentalism, notwithstanding the specific warning within Holy Scripture, of which the vital framework is prophecy. The Chief Apostle, Peter, issues the warning:

> So we have confirmation of what was said in prophecies; and you will be right to depend on prophecy... At the same time, we must be most careful to remember that the interpretation of scriptural prophecy is never a matter for the individual.

> (2 Peter 1:19–21)

In 'Scriptural Power Lines' we employed the concept of an

overhead projector as a means of understanding Holy Scripture. When reading the description of the Creation in Genesis it is not difficult to imagine we are watching an unfolding story projected in quick succession on seven slides. Having viewed the six, we might with some foreknowledge be anticipating the seventh showing the Creator having a rest. But no! – the screen is blank. On reflection we may think the slide is misplaced, but in fact we are witnessing some original Scriptural advertising – *Watch this space*.

The blank side may thus be seen as prophetic of the Second Creation or Re-creation, revealed by the birth of Paradisal Man with the Incarnation of the Son of God, Jesus, the archetype of ourselves. The Transfiguration of our Lord Jesus Christ was witnessed by chosen men from both the old order and the new, thereby indicating that the two Testaments are but one continuing order. The second does not annul the first but incorporates it, making it sacramental, thereby transforming it and uplifting it, making it glorious.

We referred earlier to the Christ as being the expressed immanence and transcendence of His Father. We now see that we are involved in this through our membership within the Body of Christ – His Church. We are commissioned to express His immanence within us which we do by our awareness in prayer and worship of His transcendence. The two are interacting. The Transfiguration further reminds us of those words of the second-century theologian, Irenaeus, to which we referred earlier, believing that man *as conceived in the mind of God* did not yet exist. From the glory of the earthly we must be transfigured to the glory of the heavenly before we can exist in the eternal kingdom.

In the relatively modern age covering the post-Renaissance/Reformation period, the reformed churches generally and the Church of England, as we know it now, in particular, have acquired both some of the misfortunes as well as the benefits of those reforms. It seems not wholly unreasonable to think that the established inclination within the Church of England towards Nestorianism may have grown out of Cartesian dualism. Nestorius emphasised the dual aspects of Jesus Christ – one human, one divine. However, there is no evidence of an intentional departure from orthodoxy, but rather of having drifted into it.

What has happened, it appears, is that over a long period we have preached a social gospel or a religionless morality, albeit in good faith. But this has had the effect of separating the Jesus of morality from the Christ of religion, whereby conduct is not related to worship. We may put this another way. At a time when only a minority of our membership is regularly worshipping, the majority have, in effect, decided to cut the cloth of Christianity to suit themselves. Thus the majority of believers follow the rules of the ethical Jesus as being the more essential way of life as they see it. The social advantages are evident. One of the greatest rhetorical preachers of the past century, Austin Farrer, warned us of the potential danger to Christianity that would follow if we 'consigned the Christ to history'. It is the Christian religion rather than its moral code that binds us unselfishly to the Christ.

We note here that one potential, if not actual, consequence of having placed too great an emphasis on Christian morality at the expense of Christian religion, was the creation of an elitist group of worshippers. This set up a moral barrier that appeared to or actually did exclude those whose need of God's grace may have been as great or greater, but who nevertheless felt excluded.

The prevailing influence of liberal humanism is not more typically emphasised than by the consensual and constant pursuit of riches and pleasures. The situation requires to be addressed by some of the harder sayings of Jesus. His comment to His disciples following the departure of the rich young man was:

> My children, how hard it is to enter the kingdom of God! It is easier for a camel to pass through the eye of a needle than for a rich man to enter the kingdom of God.
>
> (Mark 10:23–26)

The consternation of His disciples was met with the reminder that, whilst it is impossible for man, with God all things are possible. Earlier in His ministry, Jesus also said:

> Enter by the narrow gate, since the road that leads to perdition is

wide and spacious, and many take it; but it is a narrow gate and a hard road that leads to life, and only a few find it.

(Matt. 7:13–14)

We may consider our Lord's choice of words to have been influenced by the similarity of His own experience, upon which He may have often reflected with divine prescience and human propriety. For His Incarnation was indeed a wondrous thing, that He, Son of God, Son of Man, should be willing to be born of a mother, who was *virgo intacta*, thus entering this world by a narrow entrance and a straight way; man's entrance to the kingdom of heaven is revealed as being no less difficult.

More of our Lord's words of stringent character followed the making of a comparison between His disciples and those of John the Baptist, whose disciples fasted, whereas those who followed Jesus did not. His response was that His disciples would fast when He was no longer with them. There would seem to be an evident need for the Church's guidance on this at the present time. There are considerable spiritual benefits that proceed from following this particular command of our Lord. Fasting, which can be observed in several ways, serves to sharpen our perception of the supernatural and also to keen the edge of our awareness of the transcendent in worship – for which in particular fasting from words as far as is possible is to be recommended as a preparation.

We have already noted that our Lord Jesus Christ, perceiving the approaching end of His earthly ministry, took deliberate action by turning out the money changers from the Temple precincts. Before pursuing the consequences of that action we need to go back, perhaps no more than a few days, to the occasion when he spoke to his disciples about the last things. It was a portentous moment which we generally think of as referring to His second coming and the end of the world. Whilst that idea cannot be excluded, our Lord's words were in one sense to be fulfilled within a short time. His coming again when it happened would be swift; we must therefore be aware. He spoke of two men in a field and two women at the grinding wheel making flour for baking. In each case one was taken and one was left. Our Lord is reminding us that the judgement that is made of us is of our own determining. Thus it happened when on the Cross of

Calvary that our Saviour, crucified between criminals, turned to the penitent thief saying, 'Today thou shalt be with me in Paradise.' But the unrepentant was left.

Finally our Lord's action in the Temple precincts achieved its purpose in attracting a crowd to hear Him telling His last parable in which He, the son of the owner of the vineyard, becomes the victim of the stewards. Tragically it is the parable of our own times.

Indeed, this parable is paradigmatic of much of the modern world, Christian and non-Christian. The entrepreneurs, developers, contractors and the heads of commerce all refuse to respond to the prophets of Greenpeace and Friends of the Earth. Instead, we have on the one hand, a worldwide destruction or consumption of the earth's natural resources, at an alarming rate and to an unsustainable degree; on the other, we have an aggressive and relentless competitiveness both in manufacturing and in commerce. This places enormous pressures, not only on those closely involved in the processes, but also on the general public, who are the intended beneficiaries and the purchasing consumers.

What develops from this, overall, is what we see today – a society of dissatisfied people who are constantly being encouraged in the belief that the quality of life is determined solely by material possessions and opportunities. Were that not a false premise upon which to base our lives, we would not experience dissatisfaction. It exposes the lie as to our true nature and reminds us that we need to attend to our spiritual qualifications.

If we do not attend to this we shall be, albeit indirectly, like those stewards in the parable, who refused to recognise the claims of the Son of God, the Christ, either upon themselves or upon the vineyard, thereby fulfilling the paradigm.

There is a wealth of evidence, in the Holy Scriptures and elsewhere, that Christlikeness or godliness gives the greatest contentment.

> Religion, of course, does bring large profits, but only to those who are content with what they have…
>
> (1 Tim. 6:6)

An intelligent and full contentment elevates the soul above all the world, and makes it angelical.

(Thomas Traherne, *The Way to Blessedness*, p.238)